# A Valley Journal

## Surviving Bereavement

### Abi May

A Valley Journal

## Onwards and Upwards Publishers
Berkeley House, 11 Nightingale Crescent,
Leatherhead, Surrey, KT24 6PD.
**www.onwardsandupwards.org**

ISBN:              978-1-907509-99-5
Typeface:          Sabon LT
Graphic design:    Leah-Maarit

Unless otherwise indicated, all scriptures are in the New King James Version. Copyright © 1982 by Thomas Nelson, Inc. Used by permission. All rights reserved.

Scriptures marked WEB are from the World English Bible.

Every effort has been made to authenticate the origin of quotations and obtain the permission of authors where quotations are not in the public domain. We apologise for any unintentional oversights and will be happy to rectify them in any future reprint and/or edition of this book.

# About the Author

Abi May was born in the south of England, of Russian/Polish ancestry. Her conversion to Christianity as a young adult was a defining point in her life and the motivation for spending twenty-five years in the Indian Subcontinent,  Middle East and Eastern Europe, where she taught and supported others in their faith walk. She now lives with her husband John in Staffordshire.

An experienced teacher of English (qualified with PGCE and CELTA), over the years Abi developed a talent for creative writing and editing. She has compiled and edited ten anthologies to date, with over 100,000 copies in circulation, and regularly publishes inspirational articles. Her work has largely centred on faith-based themes, although she also sits on the management board of a local health charity and does other volunteer work.

The tragedy of losing both of her children prematurely has had an overarching impact on Abi's life, and much of her focus is now on bereavement support.

Author's website:        *www.abi.mayihelp.co.uk*
Author's email address:    *abi@mayihelp.co.uk*

3

# Dedication

In loving memory of my two children

## Pax

### 1979-1982

*A cheerful child,
with a gentle spirit.*

## Catherine

### 1980-2011

*A beautiful young woman,
a kind and generous friend.*

Rest in peace until we meet again.

*"The eternal God is your
dwelling place."*

**Deuteronomy 33:27**

# Contents

# A Valley Journal

# Foreword by Joanne Speed

We live in the Western world where topics such as death, dying and bereavement are still not easily discussed, despite all our modern advances. There is little in life that prepares us for the loss of those people most dear to us, whether through a prolonged decline in health or terminal illness, or the shock and trauma experienced through sudden or accidental death. We find ourselves immersed in a confusing world of death certification, funeral planning, potential inquests, probate, and afterwards the road less travelled of grief, loss and often isolation and loneliness.

"Grief is the price we pay for love," commented Dr Colin Murray Parkes OBE, a leading international speaker and writer in the field of bereavement and loss. It is wonderful to celebrate life and love, but we are not so good at commemorating and capturing our thoughts, memories and emotions around the things and people that we have lost, which have been so very important to us. We may brush our feelings aside as we strive to be stoical or to support those people also affected.

*A Valley Journey: Surviving Bereavement* can help the reader to explore these memories, emotions and thoughts around their bereavement experience, and at different stages of the bereavement journey. It gives an opportunity for time and space to capture the importance of the person they have lost, to understand why they feel such emotional pain, but throughout providing short pieces of poetry and meditations to help uplift the reader and to draw out the sting of death and loss. It may help some readers to work through this book section by section, or to share parts of it with others, to work with a professional counsellor alongside them, or to keep it as a private journal that can be later reflected upon to understand how far they have come on their bereavement journey.

Abi May speaks from her own heart and experiences to help guide others through their individual journeys, and her depth of understanding and compassion speaks volumes as the pages are turned. This is an emotional book to work though; more tears may well be shed as the journey of recovery continues. As a professional bereavement and loss counselling and support service, we hope that this book will help all readers as they process their own individual experience of grief and that it will provide opportunities for personal growth and understanding as it enables people to become more resilient in coming to terms with their loss.

**Joanne Speed**
CEO, The Dove Service[1]
November 2013

---

[1] The Dove Service, BACP Accredited Counselling Service; www.thedoveservice.org.uk

# Preface

*B*ereavement is not an easy journey, particularly if you have suffered the loss of someone close to you. *A Valley Journal* is based on a collection of original writings, inspirational reflections and poems, alongside quotations and scripture portions. It includes suggestions for putting your own thoughts and feelings into words, so that this book can become the basis of a personal reflective journal.

This book is not a step-by-step guide to surviving bereavement; it is based on my personal experiences as a bereaved mother, along with extensive reading. No two journeys through grief are identical, yet we can find comfort in discovering that what we are experiencing is not entirely unique.

When you are seeking comfort, strength and hope, dip into this book. There is no need to follow a particular order. Look at the headings and see what appeals; read a page here or a page there as your concentration permits. Make your own notes, when you are ready, and if you wish. Return to the book later on; I think you will be surprised to discover how far you have travelled.

### THE VALLEY OF THE SHADOW

This chapter centres on the grief and difficulties of coping with the new reality of life without your loved one, particularly in the initial period following your loss. It includes a number of suggestions for personal reflection.

### THE JOURNEY THROUGH

This continues the interactive theme of the previous chapter, with readings and suggestions offering support as you gradually adjust to life without your loved one.

### THE LOSS OF A CHILD

A parent who has experienced the loss of a child is widely acknowledged as facing one of the most difficult bereavements. A child lost through miscarriage or stillborn; lost in early infancy or childhood; lost in their teens or young adulthood; lost in later years – the age makes little difference. This chapter seeks to bring solace to parents who have lost one or more sons or daughters.

### REFLECTIONS IN THE VALLEY

Here you will find readings, reflections and prayers based on the Christian faith, to support and comfort you on your journey.

## RESOURCES

At the back of the book you will find information about helpful organisations, along with guidance for those wishing to support the bereaved.

www.avalleyjournal.co.uk

**My pen, your pen**

*Sometimes the sadness is so deep*
*I cannot find the tears to weep.*
*Then I take a pen into my hand*
*And see if my notebook will understand.*

 **Whenever you see this symbol, you are invited to reflect and add your own thoughts.**

# Introduction

"We understand death for the first time when he puts his hand upon one whom we love."

*Madame De Staël*
*Swiss author (1766–1817)*

*I*t was a warm and sunny April morning. A rapid sequence of phone calls was followed by a car journey that seemed to last forever. The next moments are fixed in my memory: arriving at noon at my adult daughter's house, standing in its shadow whilst being informed that she was there but "gone", falling to the ground and crying hysterically, and finally in that haze of agonising, bewildering sorrow, quoting the words of Psalm 23:4: "Yea, though I walk through the valley of the shadow of death, I will fear no evil, for You are with me."

I had always understood this scripture to be God's comfort during the time of our own death; but in the days that followed, the words took on a new meaning. I had been in the valley of death; not my own, but my daughter's. I had been there before, when my son had died in infancy, twenty-nine years earlier. This is the valley that no parent wants to pass through – the place of our worst nightmares, a place of great darkness.

No matter what one's belief about life after this life, there is still pain in losing someone we love. Not having their presence in this world is a loss on many levels, and it is difficult to learn to live without them. Rather like losing an arm or a leg, although the wound may heal, we are still hobbling through life without a limb. We are told, "Blessed are they who mourn, for they will be comforted." (Matthew 5:4) The comfort does come, but it does not come all at once.

I have been working on this book while I journey through the valley of grief, seeking to survive. It is written in a way that I hope will be helpful to others.

The psalmist proclaimed to the Lord, "You are with me." No matter how lonely our journey seems, we have a friend in the valley. May He walk with us through the shadows, out into the light.

**Abi May**
Staffordshire, England

# PART ONE

# The Valley of the Shadow

## The First Days

> "Even though I walk through the valley of the shadow of death..."
>
> *Psalm 34:4*

*Y*ou're here because you've lost someone who was important to you: man or woman, adult, child or baby; old or young; husband, wife, partner or lover; friend or associate; son, daughter, brother, sister, mother, father, or other relative.

No matter who they are or what your relationship has been to them, they are no longer living on this earth.

It's a dizzy, unsettling feeling. You can't completely grasp that it is real; you wish with all your heart that it wasn't.

It's permanent. There is no changing the outcome. There is only a new reality – the reality of your life without this special someone.

You are in the valley of the shadow of death.

> *My world seemed to end today;*
> *The one I love has gone away.*

**My loved one's name:**

**Why he or she is special to me:**

# The Funeral

What could be worse? You are in no state to make decisions; you're dealing with the very worst days of your life and you're not thinking straight. But almost immediately you must decide on a course of action.

Arranging the funeral and burial or cremation cannot be postponed. The burden may be slightly lifted; family or friends may help you prepare, taking some of the burden of organisation out of your hands, or you may share the responsibility with someone close to you. Or you may find yourself entirely responsible.

In any event, proceedings will be organised in reference to your religion, culture and circumstances. 'Celebrating a life' is one outlook on funerals; others may have too broken a heart to consider it a celebration of any kind. Hopefully arrangements will reflect your preferences and what you feel pays respect to your loved one.

Some discover an extraordinary grace to bring them through this difficult time; others struggle to breathe. Some find they get so busy in the lead-up to the funeral that it is not until afterwards, when they are greeted by the terrible anti-climactic silence, that the reality of the disaster sinks in. This is another event to survive, another event on the journey through the valley.

*Think, O Lord, in mercy*
*On the souls of those*
*Who, so soon gone from us,*
*Now in death repose.*
*Here 'mid stress and conflict*
*Toils can never cease;*
*There, the warfare ended,*
*Bid them rest in peace.*

*Rest eternal grant them,*
*After weary fight;*
*Shed on them the radiance*
*Of your heav'nly light.*
*Lead them onward, upward,*
*To the wondrous place,*
*Where your children gather*
*To gaze upon your face.*

*E. S. Palmer*
*Adapted*

**Date and place of my loved one's funeral:**

# Breathe In, Breathe Out

"But oh! As to embrace me she inclin'd, I wak'd, she fled, and day brought back my night."

*John Milton*
*(1608–1674)*
*On his deceased wife*

*R*espite from grief is often extremely brief in the early days of bereavement. As time passes, you will likely experience increased periods of calm. Then, sometimes unexpectedly, a wave of agony passes over you once again. Your loved one is gone, never to return. The reality hits you fresh like the blast of a freezing wind in the middle of winter when you step out of the shelter of your warm home. Didn't you realise it before? Hadn't you taken it on board? Is this really the first moment you understood?

Over and over the realisation returns; this is a permanent state of affairs. He or she won't call; there will be no birthday cards; there will be no new photos of life's changing stages. There is an empty space at the table; a name missing from the Christmas card list.

The agony of their permanent absence from present life can be physically painful. It hurts, not just in the mind and figurative heart, but at times the heart beating under your ribs actually aches, your chest tightens, your pulse quickens. There may be moments of gasping for breath;

other moments when you wish you could just stop breathing for a moment.

Although it does not feel like it at the time, the frequency and duration of this extreme pain will gradually recede. You can survive, as the mourners of centuries can attest; but while you're in the midst of this agony, believing in your own survival may not be easy. What is more, sometimes you may feel so wretched you are not sure that you even *want* to survive.

If you feel like this, often the best you can do is simply breathe in and out. Take life a moment at a time. Even in these most difficult moments, you are not alone. You have a Friend.

> *Where the mourner weeping*
> *Sheds the secret tear,*
> *God His watch is keeping,*
> *Though none else be near.*
>
> *God will never leave thee,*
> *All thy wants He knows,*
> *Feels the pains that grieve thee,*
> *Sees thy cares and woes.*

*Heinrich S. Oswald (1751–1834)*

21

**Aspects of my life that are most changed since my loved one died:**

## Memories

*M*y loved one died. That was a moment of time. But more important, my loved one *lived*. She moved, breathed, experienced life. She ate, she drank, she worked, she slept. She laughed, she cried, she spoke, she listened. She read, she wrote, she sang, she loved. She lived for not merely a single moment, but many moments.

There is so much more to focus upon than the moment of his or her passing. There is a life to celebrate, however short or long.

> *Flashes of memories*
> *Pinpricks of light*
> *In the dark sky of night.*
>
> *Rewind the memories*
> *Moments of time*
> *When happiness was mine.*
>
> *Savour the memories*
> *All that remains*
> *Of life that was gained.*
>
> *Cherish the memories*
> *For in them we keep*
> *Their souls – our friends who sleep.*

**Today I want to say thank you
for the happy memory of...**

## He Counts, She Counts

"The very hairs of your head are all numbered. Do not fear therefore; you are of more value than many sparrows."

*Luke 12:7*

*On the news they proclaim*
*The world's population has gained*
*The total of seven billion.*

*If my daughter was still here*
*It would be a full*
*Seven billion and one.*

*If my son was still living*
*The total they'd be giving*
*Is seven billion and two.*

*And for you, the reader, bereaved*
*The total you would no doubt prefer*
*Is seven billion and three.*

*Of course the numbers are not exact*
*And what I'm writing is not quite fact*
*Except that we miss each and every one.*

Each one is an individual. Each one counts. Here's something unique about my loved one that I am proud to recall:

## Grieving

"My face is flushed from weeping, and on my eyelids is the shadow of death."

*Job 16:16*

*Waking confused at a world still turning,*
*Pain in heart, a constant yearning;*
*This is grieving.*

*Not wanting to get up this morning,*
*Exhausted with sorrowing;*
*This is grieving.*

*Sitting lonely, without speaking,*
*Not having much interest in eating;*
*This is grieving.*

*So much time spent in thinking,*
*Thoughts are sad, vainly racing;*
*This is grieving.*

*Stomach aches, a sinking feeling*
*From reality, soul is reeling;*
*This is grieving.*

*Still alive, but barely breathing,*
*Wishing for a break from feeling;*
*This is grieving.*

## A Valley Journal

*A loss so great that words are failing,*
*Can't express just how it's paining;*
*This is grieving.*

*Time isn't speeding but slowing,*
*Can't be turned back, just keeps going;*
*This is grieving.*

*Mouth dry, hands cold, just sitting,*
*For something unknown waiting;*
*This is grieving.*

*Head bowed low, tears are falling,*
*Heart for hope is vainly calling;*
*This is grieving.*

*In the shadows, sit remembering,*
*Tears and memories without ending;*
*This is grieving.*

*In the silence, sitting listening*
*For a voice, a quiet whispering;*
*This is grieving.*

*Getting up each new morning,*
*Although it hurts, the world is turning;*
*This is grieving.*

*Cleaning house and doing washing,*
*Writing emails and going shopping;*
*Still it's grieving.*

**I miss you, my loved one, because...**

# Sudden Death: The Day the Earth Stood Still

*I*n the morning the sun rose. You woke. It was just an average day, with no outstanding expectations. But by the time the sun went down in the evening, the earth had stopped moving.

In the evening the sun set. You retired for the night, hoping for a peaceful sleep. But before the sun rose again, the earth had stopped moving.

You weren't expecting anything different to happen this day. You had said no goodbyes, made no preparations, had no expectation of disaster. But disaster did strike. By reason of an accident, sudden health crisis, suicide or murder, your loved one lost their life.

The slow lead up to death that precedes a terminal illness is difficult to bear, yet it affords some period of adjustment; there are usually at least some possibilities for you to say goodbye mutually, to talk about what needs to be talked about, to make preparations emotionally and practically for your loved one's departure. This isn't always the case, as your loved one may have lost consciousness, or an illness that did not seem serious can suddenly take a turn for the worse. So even with a 'gradual' decline, there can still be a great shock.

However, sudden death has no preparation period whatsoever. It is traumatic and life-changing. The world has not stopped turning, but it may seem as though it has. And when the sun rises again the following day – the new day, the first day that will run its course without the living presence of your loved one – the feeling of shock and disbelief may increase. It can be quite surprising to your shattered sensibilities that everybody else is going on with their normal daily activities. Don't they realise? Don't they get it?

Surviving the sudden death of a loved one is not unlike surviving a physical accident. It is a profound shock to your system, and just as a physical shock may leave you chilled and shaking, so this emotional shock may have physical impact. Staying warm, having warm drinks and eating small nutritious meals or snacks, even if you don't feel much like eating, are a good idea.

You will never forget the moment of discovery. If it was a phone call or a knock on the door, it may take many months before your heart does not skip a beat at the sound of the phone or the doorbell. If you discovered your loved one, the flashbacks may be intense for a long time to come.

It is likely you will endlessly replay the events of that day. According to experts, this is healthy, as it gives your mind an opportunity to come to terms with the reality of what has happened.

It is just as likely that during the early days, it won't seem like reality; just a bad dream from which you hope beyond words to awaken. But this isn't a dream you can wake up from. It really happened. Your mouth dry, your whole body rigid with tension, perhaps a feeling of dizziness, sleepless nights, utter emotional exhaustion – all of this and more is part of your painful journey of survival.

But it is a journey of *survival.* It can be survived.

 **Lest I forget...**

# Be Kind to Yourself

"Time is the great comforter of grief, but the agency by which it works is exhaustion."

*Letitia Elizabeth Landon*
*Poet and novelist (1802–1838)*

The shock of your loved one's passing has sent you reeling emotionally and mentally. There is a physical impact also, and it is common to feel chilled and exhausted. The exhaustion may carry on for a long time.

"Be kind to yourself" is the excellent advice offered by many bereavement support services. I puzzled over this for a while; what did it mean? For each of us it may be a little different, but for me I discovered it was:

- Warm drinks
- Sitting in a quiet, warm room
- Sitting out in nature
- Watching the flowers grow
- Warm baths
- Sitting quietly
- Watching some light, not-too-serious TV
- Eating light food, such as fruit and salads
- Sitting in the sunshine
- Listening to gentle instrumental music

You will see that sitting was my predominant activity. Quietness, warmth, light and cessation of creative activity were the first ways I found to "be kind to yourself." Later on I found that non-mentally-demanding activities such as gardening, painting and crafts were very helpful as well.

Being kind to yourself means taking the time to allow yourself to recover, at your own pace. You need to recoup your strength as you reorient your life in this new place where you find yourself.

 **This is how I can be kind to myself:**

# PART TWO

# The Journey Through

## Surviving Bereavement

# The Spiral Staircase of Grief

*L*osing a very dear loved one can send you onto such a mental and emotional rollercoaster that you may sometimes feel as though you're losing your mind. But much of what you're going through is normal and expected – and this is scientifically corroborated.

Dr Elisabeth Kübler-Ross first published her seminal research 'On Death and Dying'[2] in 1969, describing five stages of attitude towards impending death. Applying equally to the bereaved, there is little contemporary literature on bereavement that does not mention these five stages. They are not linear stages – we do not pass through to the next stage, leaving the first behind – but it's more like a spiral staircase. We pass through each stage again and again, returning at different times, at different degrees.

## DISBELIEF, DENIAL AND ISOLATION

When learning of the death of a loved one, the first reaction is often denial. It feels as though it cannot be true, it cannot be real. This feeling of disbelief is strongest in the earliest days, but can reappear for a long time afterwards at unexpected moments.

---

[2] Kübler-Ross, Doctor Elisabeth. 'On Death and Dying', Tavistock, London: 1970, et al.

Disbelief is often accompanied by isolation. You may feel genuinely surprised, even insulted, that the world is going on with its normal daily business. The postman delivers the mail; the sweeper cleans the street; buses arrive and depart; the school opens its doors, the teachers teach; supermarkets are filled with shoppers; your next-door-neighbour goes out to work; your niece has a birthday; your best friend gets a promotion at work; the couple down the street celebrate the arrival of their first child; the bills come through the door. It's all carrying on just like it always has, but you're not carrying on just like you always have. You feel alone. It is a sinking, almost terrifying loneliness. You're the only one who feels this precise pain.

## ANGER AND GUILT

Anger is another phase in our journey. For the bereaved, the most difficult anger to manage may be self-directed, in the form of guilt. No matter the circumstances of your loved one's death, guilt is one of the most common reactions.

Anger less likely to be put into words can also be felt towards your loved one. You may feel deserted and rejected by their death, left alone to face life with all its challenges without their support and companionship. In addition, there may be unresolved issues between you that also carry a mixture of anger and guilt. You may feel it is too late to make things right. You may even feel guilty for feeling this way. But try to remember that anger is part of the natural reaction to bereavement. Some find comfort by writing letters to their loved one expressing their feelings, with complaints and apologies included.

Your anger may also be directed towards those on the periphery of your loved one's death, such as nursing staff, doctors, drivers on the road, other family members – just about anybody. Depending on the circumstances, there may even be some justification for feeling they could have done better, but whether there is or not, ultimately this anger must be dealt with and put to rest. Aim for forgiveness for the sake of your own well-being.

And finally, there may be anger at God. He could have changed the outcome, couldn't He? But He didn't, did He? Why? This is a question with no easy answers, and those who would respond with a trite "It was God's will" are most likely missing the point. Two bereaved sisters both made the same comment to Jesus: "Lord, if You had been here, my brother would not have died."[3] There is a tinge of an accusatory 'why' in their question. The response? He is not angry or upset; we are told, "Therefore, when Jesus saw her weeping ... He groaned in the spirit and was troubled."[4]

It is the compassion of His sorrow that reminds us that a God of love "does not afflict willingly, nor grieve the children of men"[5]. He sorrows with us, and perhaps that is the closest we can come to comfort.

---

[3] John 11:21, 32
[4] John 11:33
[5] Lamentations 3:33

"God is our refuge and strength, a very present help in trouble. Therefore we will not fear, even though the earth be removed, and though the mountains be carried into the midst of the sea; though its waters roar and be troubled, though the mountains shake with its swelling."

*Psalm 46:1-3*

## BARGAINING

Bargaining is an odd stage when related to the bereaved. While the terminally ill may try to make bargains with their doctors and/or God in hope of a reprieve, the bereaved do not have this recourse. But perhaps the bargains are more subtle. I cleaned my daughter's house, paid up her bills, tidied her things, threw out the rubbish. Now everything is sorted, she can come back, can't she? That question, unlike 'why', does have an answer, and the answer is a firm and resounding no.

There is another type of bargain. He or she is gone from this life; I'm still here, but I wish I was not. I will live, but not really live; breathe, but not really breathe; see, but not really see. I will take no pleasure from life; I will ignore the beauty and happiness that still exist in this world; I will remain in the shadows of the valley. My life has not ended, but any quality in my life has finished.

Sadly, this does not bring any resolution. Just as the tidying up of my daughter's affairs did not bring her back, nor would the denial of my own life. Well-meaning friends plead, "Let her rest in peace. This is not what she would have wanted." My unspoken response: "How do you know what she would have wanted?" So I wear black and keep the curtains of my life drawn closed.

How long will this bargain last? Some pass through their bereavement, assimilating their loss, and carry on living. Others remain in that dark place for years. Either way, the loss remains. Our loved one will not return.

I do not believe that anybody can sort out this bargain for you, nor should they impose a timetable of when you should reopen the curtains of your life. When you are able, you will. In time, hopefully, you will reach a place where your life can still be lived. It's not the life you would have chosen, for it is without the presence of the one you love, but it is life.

## DEPRESSION

Depression is a stage that few of those bereaved of a close loved one will escape. The reality of your loss has sunk in; the light of your life has gone out. Why get up in the morning to a world still turning, but turning without your loved one? Why bother? Perhaps your heart echoes the words of Job, the bereaved father in the Bible, who lamented, "Why did I not die at birth? Why did I not perish when I came from the womb? My eye will never again see good."[6]

---

[6] Job 3:11, 7:7

There are probably moments, even days, when you feel you cannot survive the grief. Life without your loved one is simply too painful. Talking and meeting with others who are similarly bereaved can be a great support and give you the encouragement you need to make it through those difficult patches. The vast majority of the bereaved do survive.

While deep sadness and elements of depression are part of the normal processes of bereavement, do not hesitate to seek professional help if the depression is persistent, unmanageable or if you are seriously contemplating ending your life. If this is how you feel, then please consult a trained counsellor or doctor for support. There are ways of surviving your grief, however unlikely or even undesirable this may seem at times.

### ACCEPTANCE

"Can I bring him back again? I shall go to him, but he shall not return to me."

*King David*
*On the death of his infant son*
*2 Samuel 12:23*

The fifth stage described by Dr Ross is acceptance. It is real. Your loved one is not coming back. For the remainder of your days, you will miss and long for them, but you will have to live without them. There is no reprieve.

Acceptance of this reality is one thing; accepting it as having been inevitable and unavoidable, or accepting that this was 'God's will' is another thing entirely. Don't confuse acceptance with agreement.

"It happened and cannot be changed; but I still do not agree that this was the best outcome, nor one that God ordained. Perhaps one day I will feel differently, but that's how I feel today." – That's the best I can personally manage as far as acceptance. Other survivors make more positive affirmations; it's wonderful if you can, but if your hurt is still deep and raw, then this reluctant acceptance of reality might have to be 'as good as it gets', at least for now.

## OTHER CONSEQUENCES OF GRIEF

Sleeplessness, loss of appetite (or, conversely, over-eating), confusion and exhaustion are some of the other common physical, mental and emotional reactions to bereavement, and they too can continue intermittently for a long time.

## A CONTINUING JOURNEY THROUGH THE SPIRAL

The stages are not linear; the bereaved do not pass neatly from one to the next and then finally 'get over it'. Rather, these stages are useful descriptions of the varying emotions of bereavement that you may or may not experience.

The loss of my daughter awakened every emotion I had regarding the loss of my son twenty-nine years earlier. I found myself weeping from the depths of my soul for him once more; weeping for the little life that was cut short. I hunted for pictures of close relatives to try to imagine what he would have looked like if he had grown up. I agonised over his last moments. In some respects, I still can't believe he's gone. It's been twenty-nine years and I'm still on that spiral staircase. Sometimes it stretches out, almost in a straight line; then it's a tight, narrow curve.

Bereavement is a process, a journey. Each one of us walks our own path and survives in our own unique way, but the general process is "common to man"[7]. Draw at least a little comfort from the realisation that what you're going through is not unusual.

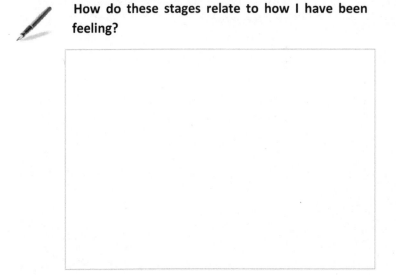

**How do these stages relate to how I have been feeling?**

---

[7] 1 Corinthians 10:13

## Moment by Moment

*A few more years shall roll,*
*A few more seasons come,*
*And we shall be with those that rest*
*Asleep within the tomb.*

*A few more suns shall set*
*O'er these dark hills of time,*
*And we shall be where suns are not,*
*A far serener clime.*

*A few more storms shall beat*
*On this wild rocky shore,*
*And we shall be where tempests cease,*
*And surges swell no more.*

*A few more struggles here,*
*A few more partings o'er,*
*A few more toils, a few more tears,*
*And we shall weep no more.*

*Horatius Bonar*
*Scottish churchman and poet (1808–1889)*

What gets you through the bad moments? Everyone is different. Some talk to a friend; others pray. Some go for a walk; others sit quietly. Some paint or write poetry; others do voluntary work and try to help others. Some look at pictures of their loved one; others try to momentarily distract themselves by reading a book or watching a film. And most of us do all of these things, and others, at different times.

What counts is not what you do, but doing anything that gets you through those difficult moments, those painful days. Tomorrow will be another day, another day to survive. What can you do today?

 **What helps me cope? What else could I try?**

# Regrets

*I*t was a crisp and sunny autumn morning. Sunday: the luxury of a day without work or responsibility, a good day for a healthy long walk, I had decided. With my mobile phone and some change in my pocket, I strode off through the suburbs of the town that was my temporary home. I knew vaguely that there'd be a craft market less than an hour's walk away, and with that as a general goal, I walked purposefully although with no great speed.

It was just a split second. My attention was distracted as I looked over to the street signs to ascertain where I was. The grass verge I was walking on was a gentle slope, not steep, but the wet grass was slick. I lost my footing and fell hard, stretching out my arms to try to break the fall. That was a mistake. I probably would have landed on the grass without much damage, but all my weight fell onto my left wrist. I gasped with pain and sat on the kerbside, head between my knees, to catch my breath. A passer-by asked if I was okay; I responded in the affirmative, but the pain in my wrist said otherwise.

To cut a long story short, I ended up in the accident department of the local hospital where I discovered that I had broken my wrist – bad news for somebody whose livelihood at the time depended on long hours of typing. After a month in a cast, the fracture mended; but even now, ten years later, on a cold or damp day, I feel an ache in that wrist, a permanent reminder of the Sunday morning walk gone wrong.

Could I have avoided the simple mishap? If I hadn't gone for the walk... If I'd gone with a friend instead of alone... If I'd worn different shoes... If I'd paid more attention to my footing... If I hadn't stretched out my arms...

Such is regret: looking back in hindsight at what we did and what we didn't do, and wishing we could change it but knowing that we can't. Even with the best of intentions, events took their course, and each event started a new string of consequences.

It is rare to pass through bereavement without times of regret: what you did or didn't do; words spoken that should have been withheld; words unspoken that should have been said. The past cannot be undone, and that realisation can be the root of our deepest regrets. It is only when we acknowledge our failures, whether real or imagined, that we can begin to find healing. Although a small ache may remain, the burning pain will gradually diminish.

And so I tell my child, "I did the best I could, at the time, with the best of intentions. I'm sorry if my best did not always bring the desired results. I'm sorry for the hurts that may have resulted. I was sometimes in the wrong place at the wrong time; I missed my footing; I was distracted; I didn't live up to my own expectations. I cannot change the past. All I can do with these regrets is give them to God and to you, my loved one, and hope that from your unseen dimension, you see, hear and forgive."

 **I'm sorry for the times I failed you. Please forgive me for...**

## Remembering Joy

*M*y daughter liked chicken. It didn't matter how it was prepared: oven-roasted chicken with a crisp brown skin, surrounded by potatoes, baked in her own small kitchen; pre-cooked cold chicken legs from the supermarket; hot fried chicken in a crunchy albeit greasy batter from the local takeaway. Chicken was something she enjoyed. So although I personally don't care much for chicken, I feel I should thank God for it.

It's a pleasant thought – something in life that gave my loved one pleasure. Something simple, something that made her happy.

We can thank God for happy moments. We can thank God for the little things that bring pleasure. We can thank God for those features of life that our loved one enjoyed.

**Some of my loved one's pleasures:**

*They are not dead,*
*Who leave us this great heritage*
*Of remembering joy.*

*They still live in our hearts,*
*In the happiness we knew,*
*In the dreams we shared.*
*They still breathe,*
*In the lingering fragrance, windblown,*
*From their favourite flowers.*

*They still smile in the moonlight's silver,*
*And laugh in the sunlight's sparking gold.*
*They still speak in the echoes of the words*
*We've heard them say again and again.*

*They still move,*
*In the rhythm of waving grasses,*
*In the dance of the tossing branches.*
*They are not dead;*
*Their memory is warm in our hearts,*
*Comfort in our sorrow.*

*They are not apart from us,*
*But part of us,*
*For love is eternal,*
*And those we love shall be with us*
*throughout all eternity.*

*Author unknown*

## Anniversaries

*T*he first anniversary approaches. In the weeks, days and hours leading up to the first anniversary, you observe the slow passing of time – the countdown is on.

I remember this time last year, blissfully unaware of what was about to happen. It is said that a veil is mercifully drawn to hide us from the future. If I had known then what was around the corner, would it have made any difference? Could I have prevented the outcome? Would I have done something differently? Of course! In retrospect, there are many things that could have been different, although whether the final outcome could have been prevented is a larger question.

But I can't turn the clock back. I can't go back to that day. The words I wished I had said are forever unspoken. The conversation I wish I could recall word-for-word has slipped from memory. The voice that I wish I could hear again is silent. The face that I wish would smile again is still. There are photographs and recordings, but they are not the same. These are reminders or tokens, but are not the essence of the person.

A year has passed. The seasons have changed. The flowers that were blooming last year at this time have long since died; new flowers have bloomed for the first time. The rain that has watered the earth, like my tears, has long since been absorbed into the ground. There is a blue sky and white puffy clouds, just like there were last year; but today they are new clouds.

The past cannot be altered. The clock is ticking. I'm watching the time. This day last year is a distant dream. So much has changed since then. I have changed so much since then. My loved one left this world, and left a gap in the fabric of my universe.

"If only I could be transported back…" It is a despairing hope. I have to accept that there is no turning back. There is no going back in time. What has happened cannot be altered.

How does one get through the first anniversary? Anniversaries are, after all, significant days. Watching the clock is probably not to be recommended, although it is the natural reaction. Starting a new tradition would be better, a personal tradition that commemorates and values the person you have lost.

This seems in keeping with Christian tradition. Easter is the major Christian festival. What do Christians do in the days leading up to this great event? They 'watch the clock'. On Palm Sunday they remember Christ's entry into Jerusalem, the Last Supper, the prayer in the garden, the betrayal, arrest and beating. Thursday moves to Friday; the time of Christ's death on the cross is marked with prayer, meditation, the taking of Holy Communion.

Lighting a candle, saying a prayer, laying flowers at the grave, posting a notice in a local newspaper or on social media, planting a tree or writing a poem, making a charitable donation or going for a memorial walk – whatever you can find to mark the anniversary that is meaningful for you is a good thing.

Mary and the other followers wept as the body of Jesus was taken down from the cross. Christians still weep, even though they know that after Friday comes Saturday, and after Saturday comes Sunday, the day of celebrating the miraculous resurrection of the Saviour. Whatever your beliefs about the afterlife, it is okay to weep. Your loved one passed from this life to the next. They are gone from your side, and that is reason to weep.

 **What could I do to mark the anniversary of my loved one?**

# Shadows

*I* am riding on a bus or a passenger in a car. I stare blankly out of the window, watching the shoppers and pedestrians as we slowly drive through the town. Suddenly, I feel a wave of disbelief: there she is, walking. Same build, same height, similar hairstyle and hair colour. Clothes somewhat similar. Surely it can't be? I can only see the back of her head, but we will drive past and then I'll look back. I know in my true mind that it can't be her, but I allow myself the glimmer of a dream.

I look back. It isn't her. Of course it isn't her. She's been dead more than a year. How could it be her?

They're like shadows, these individuals who remind us of the ones we have lost. We all experience this at times. It could be a sight or it could be a voice in a crowd. We know it can't be... but we allow ourselves the luxury of hope, even for a second.

The hope is followed by ache. It wasn't him. It wasn't her. It couldn't have been, and never will be again in this life.

Living with loss means adjusting to the world without their presence. But we still see shadows.

**This is how I remember my loved one's appearance:**

## The Waves of Grief

"God washes the eyes by tears until
they can behold the invisible land
where tears shall come no more."

Henry Ward Beecher
*Clergyman and social reformer (1813–1887)*

*Grief is as the waves of the sea.*
*Each wave builds, rises, to a peak.*
*Then crashes on the shore*
*Only to rise and crash some more.*

*Never ending sea, calm one day*
*Then turbulent again with loud waves,*
*Day in, day out, on sandy beach,*
*Continuing its relentless reach.*

*Stop, stop, I beg, I plead,*
*Can't waves stop and be at peace?*
*But still they rise, still they roar*
*Crashing out on sandy shore.*

*Some days it seems a little calm,*
*No ship today will come to harm,*
*The sea is deep, intense and blue;*
*This is a day that we'll see through.*

But then again, e'en a gentle wind
And ripples grow to waves again;
There is no stopping, no surcease,
Surf is crashing on distant reef.

There is no end, it just goes on
Through the day, and when day's done.
Waves are falling into foam
One more, one more, one more.

Grief is endless, like these waves
Unrelenting from birth to grave,
Yet as I look upon this sea
There is a thought that comforts me.

Waves continue, yet are bound,
Their limits by the shore are found.
A controlling force from up above
Keeps them held within its love.

On and on, the waves crash on,
On and on, they're never done.
Tears may fall, on we weep
Yet on these shores, love does keep.

The Love that guards the sea in place
Will surely save us by His grace.
The waves that splash in glistening foam
Will one day carry us on to home.

*Grief is endless, like the sea,*
*Waves rise and fall continually;*
*We'll bear it today and evermore,*
*Love's waves crashing upon our shore.*

 **My loss is difficult for me to cope with at the moment because...**

## Life's Intersections

*N*o matter your beliefs about the continuation of life after death, wherever your loved one is now, they are there, not here where you are. Perhaps you believe – or are told – that you should be happy that your loved one is now at peace in a better place, without pain or sorrow. But you are still here, and you miss them! Your faith may offer great comfort, but at other times it may not make much difference at all; it may even contribute to feelings of confusion. You don't have the interaction and conversation that is part of life. The pain of separation continues day after day, some days less bearable than others.

In the years preceding my daughter's death, she had lived in a different city, and we spent countless hours on the phone daily. These conversations are a treasured memory, although my days are very different now.

> *I'm waiting for my phone to ring*
> *I'm her mum, I'm listening.*
> *It's been so long since I heard her voice;*
> *Is the silence her own choice?*
>
> *Just waiting for another call*
> *To tell me what's up, and all*
> *What she bought down in the shops,*
> *Expansion of her wardrobe can't stop.*

*The news isn't always good and bright,*
*Life isn't easy, day or night,*
*But news is news, it comes in fresh,*
*Drawn again from each day's breath.*

*I'm waiting for the call, such a long wait*
*Sitting here in fanciful state*
*Just wishing for another chance to chat,*
*To talk for an hour about this and that.*

*Waiting, waiting, waiting, why do I wait?*
*She won't ring again, it's too late.*
*After all, her phone is in my drawer;*
*She doesn't use it anymore.*

 **My life intersected with my loved one. Here's a treasured memory of that intersection – something I miss but I am glad was once mine:**

# Echoes

I am sitting on a train, watching the world going by. Suddenly, I realise I'm passing through *her* station.

> *She stopped here, once,*
> *Seems so long ago.*
> *She got off the train,*
> *Took a taxi home,*
> *Called me to say,*
> *"I've arrived okay."*
> *(She won't call me today.*
> *She's gone away.)*

*E*choes. I'm looking through a second-hand book stall and come across a book we read together, many years ago... We're invited out for supper and we're served her favourite meal... I rummage through a pile of old coins; there's one dated the year when... I'm watching television and someone is wearing an outfit just like... I find an old photo that I'd forgotten I had...

In some respects these echoes are welcome. They are reminders of my loved one, moments that we shared. I cherish these echoes. But they are accompanied by yearning – the deep ache in my soul to have my loved one here at my side again. This ache cannot be fulfilled.

The emotional upheaval caused by the endless reminders of our loved one is exhausting but unavoidable.

**Here's an echo that was a pleasant surprise:**

## Setbacks and Flashbacks

*Y*ou're journeying through your grief, and feel as though you're making progress. At the beginning, every day was bad. Then you had a few days when it was somewhat bearable. Gradually, as time passed, the less-bad days started to predominate, and you even had periods when you were fairly content. You still feel as though you could never be happy again, but you surprise yourself. A meal out, a trip to a country fair, a weekend away, the discovery of a new hobby, the visit of an old friend, a good book or film, a bonus from your job – all fleeting events where you find yourself happy for moments or even hours.

And so you reach a point where you feel that you're dealing with your loss. Some days are still worse than others, but it is increasingly bearable.

Until...

You're driving down the road, and suddenly you remember that this is the road you were driving on when you returned from the scene of your loved one's passing. Your pulse quickens; you feel hot and sick. All the emotions of that day come flooding back; each word spoken echoes in your mind. You did not invite this flashback – it came to you with no invitation and no welcome – but here you are in the midst of it, reliving the very worst day of your life.

Or perhaps an old friend is dealing with issues in her own life and takes out some of her anxiety on you. She is angry with your grief; she wants you to get on with life. Probably deep down she is afraid of having to face a similar tragedy of her own. Whatever the case, in an angry outburst she insists you should 'move on'. She says that she doesn't want to hear about your loss anymore; she already knows that your loved one is dead; she doesn't need that information repeated. Many of your old friends have given you wide berth because your grief was too much for them to bear. Being ignored did hurt but nothing like the pain inflicted by these unkind words and unsolicited advice.

Or perhaps you're watching television, and the fictional portrayal of a death not unlike that of your loved one appears without notice. It's too late to look away; you've already seen it, and now you cannot avoid watching. You are glued to the screen, although you are screaming inside.

Or perhaps it's an event on the news, and you become fixated with the similarities to your own tragedy. Your heart bleeds at the thought of what the newly bereaved are going through because you know you've been there...

You've suffered a setback. Once more the weeping, once more the sleeplessness, once more the agony of mind and heart that does not seem to cease. You're back on an earlier part of the spiral road of grief. You were aware this might happen, but you're shocked by the ferocity of your feelings.

Take a deep breath. What has helped you through difficult moments before? Distraction – what about reading a book or watching television? Or perhaps some activity, like cleaning, gardening, crafts? Get out of the house, go for a walk, go shopping? Visit a sympathetic friend? Call a telephone helpline and open your heart to a stranger? Remember: be kind to yourself.

The agony of the moments will pass. Believe that you will live through them, take a deep breath, and continue on your journey.

 **What has helped me through some of my worst moments?**

# The Second Year

*Time is too slow for those who wait,*
*Too swift for those who fear,*
*Too long for those who grieve,*
*Too short for those who rejoice,*
*But for those who love, time is*
*Eternity.*

Henry Van Dyke
*Author, educator and clergyman (1852–1933)*

*T*ime passes. At the start, you counted the days. Then it was weeks, then months. The first anniversary came and went. Perhaps you'll feel better now... and for some, this is true, as the immediate agony of loss recedes into more manageable grief. But the second year is not always better, and in some respects it can be worse than the first.

Immediately after bereavement, everything can seem rather new, because it has to be faced for the first time. There was the first time you went shopping since he passed away, the first day back at work, the first time you went to that restaurant where you used to go together... There was the first birthday without her, the first Christmas, the first holiday. Painful firsts and a maelstrom of emotions mark that first year until it culminates in the anniversary.

The second year can be somewhat different. You've survived one year of firsts, and it's possible that your emotions are not quite as tempestuous as they were. But as you progress through the second year, there is a stone in the pit of your stomach, a deep weight in the bottom of your heart, a bleak cloud in your mind. There is an increasing realisation: this is permanent. You survived a year, you were as brave as you could be, but he or she is still not coming back. Ever.

The reality of the second year since I lost my daughter has been as much agony as the first, if not more so, but in a different way. My fits of crying have lessened and are now periodic rather than daily. But reality hits me over and over. Sometimes I'd almost prefer the tears to flow than this quiet agony of realisation. Reality. Never again in this life will my loved one breathe, eat, drink, walk, talk and all that living entails. Never again in this life will I see my loved one. Never again in this life will I hear my loved one's voice except as a whisper of the soul (or a recording). There is no news to tell her grandmother – how she is doing, how her work is, how her finances are. Her Facebook page is eerily quiet.

Reality is reality, and just as at any difficult moment during the first year of your bereavement, during the second year you will need to find your own ways to survive. Distraction can sometimes work: working at your job, reading a book, watching TV or a film. Physical activity can be helpful: sports, an arts or craft project, gardening, even cleaning. Going to church, praying and singing in the company of others might be an answer for some, whereas quiet contemplative walks might be better for others. You might want to try something new, like taking up a new hobby.

Keeping your loved one 'in the conversation' is important to you, although your friends may hesitate to mention his or her name, lest this provoke unwanted emotions. But do try to find a listening ear, even if it is a page in a notebook, to tell a little anecdote or recount some happy event in your loved one's life. Your history together is still your combined history, even without their immediate presence.

**This is an event in my loved one's life that I remember with a smile:**

# The Journey Through

*M*ourning and the process of grief have been aptly described as work. Adjusting to an existence that no longer contains the living presence of our loved one is a painful, lengthy and exhausting process. It is not a straightforward journey, for this is a winding valley, with a river that at times flows deep. There are dangers of rock-falls, slippery paths where we may lose our footing, and a cold and lonely wind blowing through. Just as we think we're reaching the end, we turn a corner and find the valley stretches onwards.

It is a long journey through the valley of grief, but it is a journey not a destination. We will pass through.

**Today's date:** _____

**This proves I have survived...**

_____ **years,**

_____ **months, and**

_____ **days since I lost my loved one.**

# PART THREE

# The Loss of a Child

## A Uniquely Painful Bereavement

*T*he relationship of a parent to his or her child is unique amongst all the relationships of life. The child carries his parents' genes, his parents' love, his parents' very life. Starting before birth, the child's life is intrinsically connected to its mother. From the moment of conception, it draws nourishment and grows, sheltered in the warmth of the womb. The mother meanwhile copes with fluctuating hormones, discomfort, nausea and all that accompanies pregnancy. Then there is the time of arrival. The mother undergoes physical pain while the father waits anxiously. All emotions reach their climax as one of life's greatest moments arrives – childbirth – the entrance of another living soul into our world.

And thus the cycle of caring, feeding, nurturing, sometimes worrying, starts afresh. A baby grows into a toddler; a toddler becomes a small child. Walking and talking are the earlier accomplishments, greeted with pride and pleasure by his or her parents. Soon there will be more, as the small child grows, starts schools, learns to read, write, perhaps ride a bike. The child has friends, has joys and sorrows, days of sickness and health.

Then comes the time when that small child reaches puberty, and soon there is a teenager facing many challenges: hormonal changes to cope with, friendships gained and lost, decisions about education and employment.

Still more time passes; the young adult must choose his or her path in life. The parents look on, still offering the warmth of their love, but realising that this young man or woman standing before them is their own person, with their own life to lead. For better or worse, the parents are faced with standing back, letting go; watching and supporting, offering advice and love, but no longer providing life's every nourishment.

Yet this young man or woman is still your child; still the one you have nurtured and cared for; still the one you have at times cried over, at times prayed for, at times celebrated alongside.

And if this life should end before yours, you will cry out from the depths of your soul that this is not the natural order of things. For a child to be laid in the grave before their mother or father is not how it was meant to be! The loss of a child, of any age, is not the same as the loss of a parent, a brother or sister, a friend, even a husband or wife. None of them were part of you as this child was.

The agony of losing a child, no matter their age, is unique amongst all bereavements.

**Each of my children is precious to me and holds their own place in my heart. Here is my list of the names and birth dates of each one of my children, both those still with me and those not:**

# A Sword through your Soul

*P*art of everyday conversation, there is a casual question at a social occasion or in the workplace that can pierce your soul like a dagger thrust into your heart: "Do you have any children? How many?" It could easily have been (although is probably not) what Simeon was referring to when he prophesied to Mary shortly after the birth of her son, Jesus: "Yes, a sword will pierce through your own soul."[8] As a bereaved parent, we can identify with the agony of her loss.

Now to the question. How do you answer? How many children do you have? You don't want your deceased child to be forgotten, but perhaps you will not always find it appropriate to give a complete answer. A full answer can lead to further questions and can open the floodgates of your sorrow. It may not always be the time and place to open these floodgates. So, as time goes by, you will find the right answers that you are comfortable with, and this may well vary on occasion.

What a strange world we inhabit, dear bereaved parents! Others make decisions about birthday gifts and holiday plans; we make decisions about how to tell about the loss of our child.

---

[8] Luke 2:35

## The Confusion of Losing a Child

*He left too soon,*
*    before his life had barely begun.*
*She left too soon,*
*    without life's opportunities run.*
*It does not seem fair of God to allow this.*
*I don't understand;*
*    this appears no kindness.*
*I'm trying to get it sorted*
*    in my mind and heart;*
*I'm trying to grasp why we had to part.*
*It hurts so bad, the loss of my child;*
*My emotions are tossed,*
*    like the ocean wild.*
*If you can relate to what I've written,*
*My heart goes out to you in compassion.*
*We bereaved parents are a breed apart*
*For it is our future*
*    that's been ripped apart.*

*A*s a bereaved parent, you will be at the receiving end of words of comfort, which may at times cause you additional anguish, however well intentioned. The words "I understand what you're going through" from someone who has lost a pet, a job, an elderly parent can irk rather than help. Unless they are a person of extraordinary empathy, if they haven't lost a child, they simply cannot comprehend the rawness of your grief, the utter agony of not being able to 'save' your child, the bleakness of a future without him or her. It's not usually something you can put into words; even if it is, it is unlikely you will express it. But if you want to try, here is a safe space:

**This is what I'd like to tell my friends about the agony of my loss:**

## Buried Dreams

*L*osing a child is losing a future. Whatever your expectations of what life would hold when the child was first conceived, they did not include this. If you have been left childless as the result of this bereavement, there are added complications. Will you be alone in your old age? To whom will you leave your possessions? Will you be remembered? Perhaps you have lost any possibility of seeing any 'children's children'. The sight of other parents and grandparents, even the voices of children in a playground, can depress you.

There are no easy answers. Dealing with this loss of the future is part of working through bereavement. It is not something you can change, and this makes it difficult to accept.

Dreams of the future are not what they were, but memories remain to be cherished.

Reflect on a happy memory of a first event in your child's life, such as first fluttering in the womb, their first breath, first step, first words, first birthday, first exam pass, first boyfriend/girlfriend, first job:

# Where Is My Lamb?

## QUIET REFLECTIONS

"He will feed His flock like a shepherd.
He will gather the lambs in His arm,
and carry them in His bosom."

*Isaiah 40:111*

"It is said of our Divine Redeemer, 'He
will feed His flock like a shepherd.'
And in His flock there are lambs
which can neither travel fast nor far.
And what will He do with the lambs?
'He will gather the lambs in His arm,
and carry them in His bosom.' He will
not carry them on His shoulder – the
emblem of strength; but in His bosom
– the image of tender love."

*John Angell James*
*Clergyman and writer (1785–1859)*

"The bosom, why that is the tenderest place, where we should put a poor creature that had a broken bone, and could not bear to be roughly touched.

"The bosom, that is the safest place. It makes one wish to be always a lamb, if one could always ride in that chariot. Delightful is the weakness, which casts us upon such gracious strength.

"'He carries the lambs in his bosom.' Why, that is the most honourable place. We would not put into our bosom that which was despised. We should not think of carrying there anything which was not choice and dear and exceedingly precious."

*Charles Haddon Spurgeon*
*Preacher (1834–1892)*

## Loved by an Angel

"She is gone! No longer shrinking from the winter wind, or lifting her calm pure forehead to the summer's kiss; no longer gazing with her blue and glorious eyes into a far-oft sky; no longer yearning with a holy heart for heaven; no longer toiling painfully along the path, upward and upward, to the everlasting rock on which are based the walls of the city of the Most High; no longer here; she is there; gazing, seeing, knowing, loving, as the blessed only see, and know, and love. Earth has one angel less, and heaven one more, since yesterday. Already, kneeling at the throne, she has received her welcome, and is resting on the bosom of her Saviour. If human love have power to penetrate the veil (and hath it not?) then there are yet living here a few who have the blessedness of knowing that an angel loves them."

*Nathaniel Hawthorne*
*Novelist (1808–1864)*
*Said to have been written following the loss of one of his children*

# My Child, My Prayer

"For I, the LORD your God, will hold your right hand, saying to you, 'Don't be afraid. I will help you.'"

*Isaiah 41:13 (WEB)*

Dear Lord,

I think about the rocky path I am walking on. My feet are unsteady; it would be so easy to stumble and fall down the precipice of despair. Yet I am not alone. You are holding my hand. It's a reassuring hold; it's strengthening and steadying me. That's a good thing.

But for my little lamb, You have done so much more. You have gathered up my child and are holding him next to Your heart. That is a beautiful picture of Your love, but honestly, I would rather my child was still in my arms. Why couldn't You leave him here?

For reasons I cannot fathom, You did not leave him in my care.

I hold my child deep in my heart. Dear Christ, You are also holding him close to Your heart. Our hearts are beating side by side in love for this child.

Dear Lord, please hold me steady. Give me the grace to let my lamb rest with you.

Please take care of my little one. Amen.

**This is my prayer:**

## PART FOUR

# Reflections in the Valley

## Glimmers of Hope

*Y*ou may be confused following your bereavement. No matter the depth of your belief in God, it can be a struggle to accept why God has allowed the death of your loved one. Some find their faith so shaken that they question not only His love but His very existence. Yet though we are faithless, He remains faithful.[9] Even if we stop believing in Him, He still believes in us.

In times of the deepest darkness of our grief, it can be difficult to find the words to pray, and we may feel removed from the comforter of our souls. If only we could realise that He is not dismissive of our sorrow. "Jesus wept."[10] The shortest verse in the New Testament is also one of the most profound revelations of God's love. He cares. He understands.

> "Then they cry out to the LORD in their trouble, and He brings them out of their distresses. He calms the storm, so that its waves are still. Then they are glad because they are quiet; so He guides them to their desired haven."
>
> *Psalm 107:28 30*

---

[9] 2 Timothy 2:13
[10] John 11:35

## Remember Me: A Prayer

*O Thou, from Whom all goodness flows*
*I lift my heart to Thee;*
*In all my sorrows, conflicts, woes,*
*Good Lord, remember me.*

*When trials sore obstruct my way,*
*And ills I cannot flee,*
*Then let my strength be as my day;*
*Good Lord, remember me.*

*If worn with pain, disease, and grief*
*This feeble frame should be,*
*Grant patience, rest, and kind relief;*
*Good Lord, remember me.*

*And, oh, when in the hour of death*
*I bow to Thy decree,*
*Jesu, receive my parting breath;*
*Good Lord, remember me.*

*T. Hawkes (1792)*

"O LORD, You know;
Remember me and visit me."

*Jeremiah 15:15*

"I will not forget you. See, I have inscribed you on the palms of My hands; your walls are continually before Me. – Says the LORD."

*Isaiah 49:15-16*

# Never Deserted

### A CREATIVE RETELLING OF JOHN 11:1-45

*T*hey were a tight-knit family. For reasons we are not privy to, none of them had married, so the two sisters and brother still lived under the same roof, content with their own company. Little did they realise that their world was about to be shattered.

It started innocuously enough: a slight fever, a feeling of sickness. Martha prepared the meals as usual but was worried to see her brother barely touching his food. Mary fretted. As the days passed, Lazarus grew weaker. Mary lovingly wiped his hot forehead; Martha prepared a light stew to coax him to eat.

As Lazarus tossed and turned on his bed in an uneasy, feverish sleep, the two sisters sat close to each other, whispering in the corner. Their anxiety was palpable; their efforts were not bringing any results. "We'll send a message to Jesus," they decided. "Surely He will help. He loves Lazarus."

When the message reached Jesus, His followers were surprised that, considering how much He cared for this family, He did not immediately set off for Bethany. It wasn't until two days later that He started out on the journey.

Meanwhile, Mary and Martha felt as though the bottom had fallen out of their lives. They had watched helplessly as their brother's life had ebbed away. They clutched at each other and wept as he took his last feeble breath. Wrapped in a shroud, his body, cold and stiff with death, was laid in a tomb.

The two sisters sat despondently in their home. It did not seem real. Sometimes they cried bitterly; other moments they were silent, struggling to assimilate their loss. Neither sister voiced these thoughts, but both questioned, why hadn't Jesus come to their aid? He had healed so many others; why hadn't He healed their brother?

Neighbours, relatives and members of the local synagogue gathered at their house, offering them comfort, bringing them food. While they appreciated all of this, it wasn't what they wanted. They wanted their brother back! Their hearts ached at this untimely loss.

Word came that Jesus was finally on the way. Mary sat, unmoved; the feeling of desertion was too great. But Martha, ever the more assertive of the two sisters, was determined to face Him. Her first words on meeting Him were a challenge but also an expression of faith: "Lord, if You had been here, my brother would not have died. But even now I know that whatever You ask of God, God will give You."

The conversation that ensued was remarkable.

Jesus said to her, "Your brother will rise again."

Martha said to Him, "I know that he will rise again in the resurrection at the last day."

Jesus said to her, "I am the resurrection and the life. He who believes in Me, though he may die, he shall live. And whoever lives and believes in Me shall never die. Do you believe this?"

She said to Him, "Yes, Lord, I believe that You are the Christ, the Son of God, who is to come into the world."

A seed of hope was planted in Martha's heart. She returned to call out Mary privately. They went together to see Jesus.

Mary's first words, like Martha's, indicated the depth of desertion she felt: "Lord, if You had been here, my brother would not have died."

Jesus, the son of man, wept. The two sisters knew He cared, He truly cared. Whatever they had felt up until that point, His compassion washed over their souls as a warm tide, bringing a measure of peace that they had not anticipated feeling again. Although their brother was dead, God was love, and it was His love they felt at that moment.

They were not expecting what happened next.

The tomb was a cave with a stone at the entrance. Jesus asked for the stone to be rolled away. Martha, with her usual practical sense, knew that in the four days since Lazarus had died, his body would have already started to decompose. Taking away the stone would expose them to a foul stench.

But moments later, with the stone moved away, a gripping prayer was made by Jesus to God the Father, and a loud instruction to Lazarus to "Come out!" Lazarus came walking out of the tomb, still wrapped in grave-clothes.

We can barely imagine the utter joy, the flood of relief, the exuberance of the two sisters. Their brother had been restored to life.

Here I sit, almost two thousand years later. Like Mary and Martha, I too am bereaved at the untimely passing of a very dear loved one. Like the two sisters, I sit weeping, disbelieving, aching. I too sometimes feel deserted. But I haven't been. Jesus wept. He cares. He is aware of the passing of time; He is aware of the pain. Our loved ones are resting in His love; we can too. No matter our weakness, His love is the strength to live another day. No matter our sorrow, we are never deserted. No matter our circumstances, His promise holds true: "I will never leave you nor forsake you."[11]

---

[11] Hebrews 13:5

**Although I sometimes struggle to find evidence of God's mercies during this time of loss, these are some of the ways He has taken care of me:**

## The Comforter

"The disciples found angels at the grave of him they loved, and we should always find them, too, but that our eyes are too full of tears for seeing."

*Henry Ward Beecher*
*Clergyman and social reformer (1813–1887)*

"Whatever, whomsoever you have lost, you have not lost your Jesus, your best Friend. You have His eye, His tender, watchful, provident eye upon you still; you have His ear open to your cries still; yes, you have His everlasting arms underneath you to sustain you still, for else you would sink ... To have a Friend in heaven, and such a Friend, so wise, so powerful, so faithful, so merciful, so sensibly affected with all our misery – so tender, so able, and so willing to bear and help us! – I say this is infinitely better than all the friends that ever we had or could have on earth.

*John Bunyan*
*Writer and preacher (1628–1688)*

When clouds and rain deform the sky,
    And light'nings glare around,
Amidst the dreary, cheerless scene,
    Some comfort may be found.

There will, at some far-distant spot,
    A streak of light appear,
Or, when the sullen vapours break,
    The ether will be clear.

And if the sun illumes the east,
    And sheds his gladsome ray,
Some boding mist, or passing cloud
    Will threat the rising day.

The heart rejoicing in the view,
    And dancing with delight,
Oft feels the touch of palsied fear,
    And sinks at thought of night.

So Hope's bright torch more clearly shines,
    Amidst surrounding gloom,
And, beldame Fortune vainly throws
    Her mantle o'er the tomb.

*Mary Matilda Betham*
*Poet and painter (1776–1852)*

# You Remain

"They will perish, but You remain."

*Hebrews 11:1*

*T*here are always lone hearth-fires; so many! And those who sit beside them, with the empty chair, cannot restrain the tears that will come. One sits alone so much.

There is Someone unseen, just here within reach. But somehow we don't realize His presence. Realizing is blessed, but rare. It belongs to the mood, to the feelings. It is dependent on weather conditions and bodily conditions. The rain, the heavy fog outside, the poor sleep, the twinging pain – these make one's mood so much, they seem to blur out the realizing.

But there is something a little higher up than realizing. It is yet more blessed. It is independent of these outer conditions, it is something that abides. It is this: recognizing that Presence unseen, so wondrous and quieting, so soothing and calming and warming.

Recognize His presence, the Master's own. He is here, close by; His presence is real. Recognizing will help realizing, too, but it never depends on it. More, immensely more, the Truth is Presence, not a thing, a fact, a statement. Someone is present. A warm-hearted Friend, an all-powerful Lord.

And this is the joyful truth for weeping hearts everywhere, whatever be the hand that has drawn the tears; by whatever stream it be that your weeping willow is planted.

*Samuel D. Gordon*
*(1859–1936)*
*Adapted*

## On Losing a Life Partner

"She was the best friend I had on earth, but my Friend in heaven is still where He was, and He will never leave me nor forsake me."

*Philip Henry*
*Clergyman and diarist (1631–1696)*
*Writing of Lady Puleston, who died in 1658*

*I* can see two pilgrims treading this highway of life together, hand in hand – heart linked to heart. True, they have had rivers to ford, and mountains to cross, and fierce enemies to fight, and many dangers to go through; but their Guide was watchful, their Deliverer unfailing, and of them it might truly be said, "In all their suffering He also suffered, and He personally rescued them. In His love and mercy He redeemed them. He lifted them up and carried them through all the years."

Mostly, they went on their way singing... But, at last, they came to a place on the road where two ways met; and here, amidst the terrors of a storm such as they had never before encountered, they parted company – the one being caught up to the invisible glory – the other, battered and bruised by the awful tempest, henceforth toiling along the road – alone. But the "goodness and mercy" which, for so many years, had followed the two travellers, did not leave the solitary one; rather did the tenderness of the Lord "lead on softly," and choose green pastures for the tired feet, and still waters for the solace and refreshment of His trembling child.

*Susannah Spurgeon*
*Wife of Charles Haddon Spurgeon (1832–1903)*
*Abridged*

"Surely goodness and mercy shall follow me all the days of my life: and I will dwell in the house of the LORD for ever."

*Psalm 23:1*

*I hold it true, whate'er befall;*
*I feel it, when I sorrow most;*
*'Tis better to have loved and lost*
*Than never to have loved at all.*

*Lord Alfred Tennyson*
*Poet Laureate (1800–1892)*

# A Silent Chamber

## By John Macduff

"God shall wipe away all tears from their eyes, and there shall be no more death, neither sorrow, nor crying, neither shall there be any more pain – for the former things are passed away."

*Revelation 21:4*

The trial may have overtaken with appalling suddenness. The hurricane may have swept your loved one down in the midst of brightest sunshine. The summons may have come at the time when the joy of your heart could be least spared; when most prized, most needed.

It may have been a cherished life, rich with the promise of usefulness. It would seem as if some anticipated piece of music had scarce its prelude or overture played, when the voices in a moment ceased; the music is hushed, the lights are extinguished; the program only begun when ended. With the drooping and blighting of that tender flower, your present feeling is...

> *There's not on earth the living thing*
> *To which the withered heart can cling.*

How altered your feelings amid the world's familiar din and bustle! The un-sympathizing crowd, all unconscious of what is transacting within your threshold, are hurrying by as before. They are exchanging with one another the same joyous recognitions, they are clad in the same gay attire, the same merry chimes mark the passing hour; and yet, to you, all is sickled over with enduring sadness; every scene and association which whispers gladness to others wakes no response but that of sorrow in your heart.

The silent chamber! It echoes to your lonely voice.

The happy fireside circle! There is a vacant seat.

The favourite walk, the cherished haunt! The smile that made it so is gone.

Ah, life has indeed become like the "flat, bare, oozy tide-mud, when the blue sparkling wave, with all its company of gliding boats and white-winged ships, the music of oars and chiming waters, has gone down"[12].

Your mind is filled with ten thousand conflicting feelings, to which you dare not give utterance; the holy visions of the past flitting before you like shadows on the wall; the future all darkness and mystery. Your pining spirit, in the first gush of its bitterness, turns away, refusing to be comforted; the feelings of an old sufferer are too truthfully the transcript of your own. "Call me not

---

[12] Harriet Beecher Stowe (1811–1896)

Naomi; call me Mara, for the Almighty has dealt very bitterly with me."[13]

Though I have dwelt on the depth of your bereavement, I do not write to aggravate your sorrow. My design is rather to solace.

A little while and the night of weeping will be over, and a gentle hand in a tearless world will dry up the very source of tears. "There is no night *there*"[14] nor any bereavement to be experienced or dreaded!

Every day is bringing you nearer that blissful reality, nearer reunion with the glorified, nearer Him who is now standing with the hoarded treasures of eternity in His hand and the hoarded love of eternity in His heart! One brief moment there will banish in everlasting oblivion all the pangs and sorrows of the valley of weeping!

"When you have passed," says a man of God who is now realizing the truth of his own words, "to the other side of that narrow river, to which we shall so shortly come, you will have no doubt that all you have undergone was little enough for the desired end."

> "Keep yourselves in the love of God, looking for the mercy of our Lord Jesus Christ unto eternal life."
>
> *Jude 1:21*

---

[13] Ruth 1:20
[14] Revelation 22:5

# Lilies of Hope

*I used to like the scent of lilies*
*And they were your favourite blooms.*
*We bought them to adorn your casket;*
*Perfume filled the room.*

*Each lily now is a teardrop*
*Leaving my heart, entering the soil*
*For that's where they laid my daughter,*
*Yes you, my precious girl.*

*The scent of lilies, fragrant, sweet*
*Is not something I can now stand*
*For it's the memory it evokes*
*Of holding your cold, still hand.*

*Can you still smell the lilies?*
*Please tell me if you can*
*For then I'd know that you still live,*
*Though how I do not understand.*

*If you can smell the lilies*
*Then their fragrance, soft and sweet*
*Will no longer be a cloud upon me*
*But a promise we'll one day meet.*

# Life, Death, and Life Once More

"Not lost, but gone before."

*Matthew Henry*
*Nonconformist minister (1662–1714)*

*M*editating on the life beyond is not a total panacea for the agony of grief, as your heart aches to have your loved one's presence in the here and now, not only in the ethereal future. But sometimes the thought of once more being in the presence of the one you have lost is a glimmer of light, illuminating the darkness of the valley.

*Then we shall rise*
*And view ourselves with clearer eyes*
*In that calm region where no night*
*Can hide us from each other0s sight.*

*Henry King*
*Poet and bishop (1592–1669)*

*Life is real! Life is earnest!*
*And the grave is not its goal;*
*Dust thou art, to dust returneth,*
*Was not spoken of the soul.*

*Henry Wadsworth Longfellow*
*Poet and educator (1807–1882)*

*W*e picture death as coming to destroy; let us rather picture Christ as coming to save. We think of death as ending; let us rather think of life as beginning – and more abundantly so. We think of losing; let us think of gaining. We thinking of parting, let us think of meeting. We think of going away; let us think of arriving. And as the voice of death whispers, 'You must go from earth,' let us hear the voice of Christ saying, 'You are but coming to Me!'

*N. Macleod*
*Bishop Brent (1862–1929)*

*I*t appears to me impossible that I should cease to exist, or that this active, restless spirit, equally alive to joy and sorrow, should be only organized dust – ready to fly abroad the moment the spring snaps, or the spark goes out, which kept it together. Surely something resides in this heart that is not perishable – and life is more than a dream.

*Mary Wollstonecraft*
*Writer and women's advocate (1759–1797)*

*I* am standing upon that foreshore. A ship at my side spreads her white sails to the morning breeze and starts for the blue ocean. She is an object of beauty and strength, and I stand and watch her until at length she hangs like a speck of white cloud just where the sea and sky come down to mingle with each other.

Then someone at my side says, "There! She's gone!"

"Gone where?"

"Gone from my sight, that's all."

She is just as large in mast and spar and hull as ever she was when she left my side; just as able to bear her load of living freight to the place of her destination. Her diminished size is in me, not in her. And just at that moment when someone at my side says, "There! She's gone!" there are other eyes watching her coming and other voices ready to take up the glad shout, "Here she comes!"

And that is dying.

*Bishop Brent (1862–1929)*
*Similar passages are attributed to Henry van Dyke and Victor Hugo*

# Transformation

"The seed dies into a new life, and so does man."

*G. Macdonald*

"Science has found that nothing can disappear without a trace. Nature does not know extinction. All it knows is transformation. If God applies the fundamental principle to the most minute and insignificant parts of the universe, doesn't it make sense to assume that He applies it to the masterpiece of His creation – the human soul? I think it does."

*Wernher von Braun*
*Rocket scientist and aerospace engineer (1912–1977)*

"The spirit of man, which God inspired, cannot together perish with this corporeal clod."

*John Milton*
*Poet (1608–1674)*

*S*omeone will say, "How are the dead raised up? And with what body do they come?" What you sow is not made alive unless it dies. And what you sow, you do not sow that body that shall be, but mere grain – perhaps wheat or some other grain. But God gives it a body as He pleases, and to each seed its own body.

So also is the resurrection of the dead. The body is sown in corruption, it is raised in incorruption. It is sown in dishonor, it is raised in glory. It is sown in weakness, it is raised in power. It is sown a natural body, it is raised a spiritual body. There is a natural body, and there is a spiritual body.

Now this I say, brethren, that flesh and blood cannot inherit the kingdom of God; nor does corruption inherit incorruption. Behold, I tell you a mystery: We shall not all sleep, but we shall all be changed – in a moment, in the twinkling of an eye, at the last trumpet. For the trumpet will sound, and the dead will be raised incorruptible, and we shall be changed. For this corruptible must put on incorruption, and this mortal must put on immortality. So when this corruptible has put on incorruption, and this mortal has put on immortality, then shall be brought to pass the saying that is written: "Death is swallowed up in victory. O Death, where is your sting? O Hades, where is your victory?"

Thanks be to God, who gives us the victory through our Lord Jesus Christ.

*1 Corinthians 15:35–38, 42–44, 50–55, 57*

## Face to Face

"Now we see in a mirror, dimly, but then face to face. Now I know in part, but then I shall know just as I also am known."

*1 Corinthians 13:12*

*Brief life is here our portion;*
*Brief sorrow, short lived care;*
*The life that knows no ending,*
*The tearless life, is there.*

*There grief is turned to pleasure;*
*Such pleasure as below*
*No human voice can utter,*
*No human heart can know.*

*And after fleshly weakness,*
*And after this world's night,*
*And after storm and whirlwind,*
*Are calm, and joy, and light.*

*And He, whom now we trust in,*
*Shall then be seen and known;*
*And they that know and see Him*
*Shall have Him for their own.*

*The morning shall awaken,*
*The shadows flee away,*
*And each true hearted servant*
*Shall shine as doth the day.*

*There God, our King and Portion,*
*In fullness of His grace,*
*We then shall see forever,*
*And worship face to face.*

*Bernard of Morlaix*
*12th century Benedictine monk*
*Translated by John M. Neale (1818–1866)*

# A Prayer

*L*et us hear Jesus' voice of encouragement and love, sounding amid the stillness of the death-chamber, and from the depths of the sepulchre, "Don't be afraid! I am the First and the Last. I am the living one who died. Look, I am alive forever and ever! And I hold the keys of death and the grave!"

O Helper of the helpless, Comforter of all who are cast down, better and dearer than the dearest and best of earthly relatives, give us that grace which You have promised specially in seasons of weakness. May we realize the truth of Your own precious promise, "As your days, so shall your strength be."[15]

May we trust Your heart, where we cannot trace Your hand. We wait patiently for the great day of disclosures, when all shall be revealed. Hear us, blessed God.

Amen.

*John MacDuff*
*Scottish author and divine (1818–1895)*
*Adapted*

---

[15] Deuteronomy 33:25

*For all the blessings life has brought*
*For all its sorrowing hours have taught,*
*For all we mourn, for all we keep,*
*The hands we clasp, the loved that sleep.*

*We thank Thee, Father; let Thy grace*
*Our living circle still embrace,*
*Thy mercy shed its heavenly store,*
*Thy peace be with us evermore.*

*Oliver Wendell Holmes*
*Poet, physician and essayist (1809–1894)*

# Afterword

*Y*ou may wonder, "Where is this journey taking me?" as you put one foot in front of the other along the trail through the valley. "If I do come out on the other side, what will I find?"

On these pages I have tried not to gloss over the very real challenges we face as we come to terms with the loss of a close loved one. Their life was precious to us, and their departure has left a hole in the fabric of our universe.

This might appear to be bleak reading, with so much discussion of the impact of grief, but it is a reality that many mourners face. Even the person of great faith who firmly believes in a life beyond will still miss the presence of the one who was important to them. If they had emigrated to the other side of the world and no longer visited, called or wrote, our hearts would ache; how much more if they have emigrated out of this world completely?

I believe that the place we are trying to reach is one of a degree of peace and acceptance. We will not remain in that quiet room of grief, with the curtains closed and our head bowed in weeping. Although it hurts, we will continue the journey of life without our loved one's visible presence. On occasion we return to the quiet room to reflect, but for the greater part of our waking hours, we are living. We will always care for our loved one, think about them, long for them and miss them – they remain close to us in our hearts and thoughts – but we accept that we cannot have them physically at our side in this life, ever again. And so we continue on life's journey.

# Coming Through

*I* shall finish here with another episode from my own story, from about thirteen months after I lost my daughter. I live with my husband on the edge of the Peak District National Park. We often explore new corners. Around six months earlier, we had gone up to the Monsal Trail, a scenic path along a ridge that follows the route of a small railway line that was closed years before. Down below, the river weaves through the valley; up on the path, the birds sing and flit amongst the wildflowers. The hills are covered with trees and lush grass; in the distance are meadows with lambs bleating.

But at times the trail leads through the dark tunnels that are part of the former railway route. Just a hundred feet of tunnel was an insurmountable barrier for me on that occasion, a relatively short time after my daughter's departure. I simply could not step into the darkness; I was overwhelmed with the feeling of uncertainty and claustrophobia. I could not walk through and had to turn back. Yet when I tried the same walk seven months later, I entered and walked through the tunnel with no real difficulty and was able to complete the walk.

How symbolic! In the same way, I discovered I had actually progressed on the journey of grief, despite not feeling like much had changed. This is my story.

*It happened to me yesterday.*
*I realised for the first time,*
*I might just survive.*
*So believe it or not,*
*On this occasion I think*
*I'll write something a bit upbeat.*

*Up in the Peak District hills*
*Weaves the Monsal Trail;*
*Formerly for trains,*
*Now it's an eight-mile path.*
*You can walk, cycle, enjoy the view*
*On a sunny day; it's nice to do.*

*My first visit last year*
*Was a very short walk –*
*Coming to a tunnel,*
*Peering into the darkness.*
*I couldn't go in, turned back;*
*That was a step too far.*

*My second visit was yesterday –*
*Started the walk, all went fine,*
*Arrived again at the tunnel.*
*People were walking out;*
*They'd been through, and then I knew*
*I too could venture inside.*

*One foot in front of the other*
*I walked into the cool shade;*
*Overhead lights, not total darkness;*
*Breathing deeply, not sure I could.*
*But those others had come through;*
*Surely I could make it too?*

*I called Catherine's name.*
*Her voice echoed in the shadows.*
*I kept walking, step by step.*
*The tunnel curved, then I saw*
*Light at the end of this path*
*I was coming through.*

*Back in the light, I felt quite proud*
*I had managed the route.*
*A path so many trod with ease*
*Had challenged me on my road of grief,*
*Yet I had come through.*
*I will come through.*

*– And so can you.*

# Resources

"Give sorrow words. The grief that does not speak, whispers the o'erfraught heart, and bids it break."

*William Shakespeare*
*Poet and playwright (1564–1616)*

You may find that speaking with those who are similarly bereaved, or simply finding a compassionate, listening ear, can be invaluable. Here is a short list of support organisations. Follow links on their websites to find national and local branches. Some host support days, local groups, internet forums and/or provide helplines.

### INTERNATIONAL ORGANIZATIONS

<u>The Compassionate Friends</u>

USA:  *www.compassionatefriends.org*
UK:   *www.tcf.org.uk*

Support for families after a child (of any age) dies. This is well-established international network that hosts websites, internet forums, support groups and helplines.

Page with links to chapters in Australia, Belgium, Canada, France, Germany, Netherlands, Philippines, South Africa and Switzerland:

*http://www.compassionatefriends.org/resources/International-Support-Related-Organizations/international_support.aspx*

## Survivors of Bereavement by Suicide

*www.uk-sobs.org.uk*

This is a self-help organisation that aims to meet the needs and break the isolation of those bereaved by the suicide of a close relative or friend. The website contains helpful resources.

Page with links for support in the USA and Australia:

*http://www.uk-sobs.org.uk/useful_websites.htm*

## Befrienders Worldwide, with Samaritans

*www.befrienders.org*

Offering confidential support and a listening ear, with helplines in 40 countries.

## United Kingdom

### Cruse Bereavement Care

*www.crusebereavementcare.org.uk*

"Somewhere to turn when someone dies." Cruse offers support following any type of bereavement, with useful information on their website, a telephone helpline and the possibility of face-to-face support.

Helpline in the UK: 0844 477 9400

### Child Death Helpline

*www.childdeathhelpline.org.uk*

For anyone affected by the death of a child of any age, from pre-birth to adult, under any circumstances, however recently or long ago.

Freephone in the UK:           0800 282 986
Freephone from UK mobile:   0808 800 6019

### The Compassionate Friends

*www.tcf.org.uk*

Helpline in the UK, always answered by a bereaved parent.

0845 123 2304 (daily 10 am – 4 pm; 7 pm – 10 pm)

## Survivors of Bereavement by Suicide

*www.uk-sobs.org.uk*

Helpline in the UK:      0844 561 6855 (9 am – 9 pm daily)

## Samaritans

*www.samaritans.org*

24-hour helpline offering confidential support and a listening ear when you need them most.

08457 90 90 90

## The Dove Service

*www.thedoveservice.org.uk*

The Dove Service offers counselling, training and support to all those affected by bereavement, life-changing illness and significant loss. Based in Stoke-on-Trent and working throughout the North West and Midlands.

01782 683155

## A Church Near You

A church is often an ideal quiet place for prayer and meditation. Also, many churches host bereavement support groups or coffee mornings.

# For Friends and Family of the Bereaved

*He that is your friend indeed,*
*He will help you in your need:*
*If you sorrow, he will weep;*
*If you wake, he cannot sleep;*
*Thus of every grief in heart*
*He with you does bear a part.*

*Richard Barnfield*
*Poet (1574–1620)*

Perhaps you've picked up this book because your friend or family member has lost someone close to them. You want to support them, but you don't always know what to say or do. Here are some thoughts that may help.

Each bereavement is unique. The personality of the bereaved, their relationship to the person they lost, events preceding the bereavement and the manner of the person's death are just a few of the many variables. Nobody grieves quite the same, and even the same person will likely grieve differently for different losses at different junctures of their life.

All of this means that none of us can truly put ourselves into that person's place. No matter how much we sympathise, comments such as "I know what you're going through" are not always helpful.

Another phrase to avoid is "Life goes on…" It doesn't for their loved one who has died, at least not in the context of this present world. A phrase like this may cause the bereaved to feel that you simply do not grasp the extent of their pain at the gaping hole left by the departure of their loved one.

Adjusting to life without the presence of a son, daughter, life partner or other significant person is not usually a quick process. This loss, after all, involves many aspects of the bereaved one's life, over and above the emotions. The widow or widower will suffer the loss of companionship, compounded by practical consequences. The parent who has lost a child has lost some of their dearest dreams and expectations for the future. The loss is permanent. That is why 'adjusting to the loss' is a more helpful concept than 'moving on'.

Try not to measure the bereaved person by your own expectations. Perhaps they sometimes seem to be immersed in their misery, avoiding normal daily activities and social events, sitting around, looking at pictures, crying aimlessly. Or perhaps they appear to be carrying on as though nothing has happened; they're busy all the time, in constant motion, taking barely any break from work. These are two extremes, and the bereaved usually fit somewhere in the middle, varying at different times between the 'mournful' and 'keeping busy'. Everyone is different; each bereavement is different, and each one finds their way through in their own way and time.

Don't expect the bereaved to 'return to normal' according to a set timetable. And don't be surprised if they seem cheerful one day, but the next they are sunk low again in deepest grief. The journey through grief is spiral, not a straight line.

Try not to be offended if you are the unexpected focus of an angry outburst. Anger is a feature of the grief process. What could be more frustrating than wishing with all of your heart that your loved one was still here, still in your presence, and not being able to do anything at all to make that come to pass?

So what can you do to support your bereaved friend? Be ready to listen when they want to talk. Give them space to grieve privately, if this is what they wish, but ensure that they don't feel forgotten. Pick up the phone and call them; don't always wait for them to call. Share happy memories of their loved one. Bring them some shopping and a cooked meal if they're not getting out of the house. Pop in for a cup of tea. Give them a hug. Oh yes, listen. That cannot be emphasised enough. When the bereaved wants to talk, give them an opportunity.

Be aware of significant dates. Anniversaries, birthdays (of their loved one and their own), Christmas and the New Year can be particularly difficult, especially in the earliest years but even for decades onwards, in fact to the end of their natural life. Sending a card, paying a visit, bringing a bunch of flowers or giving a call are all simple ways of letting your bereaved friend know that their pain is not forgotten. And throughout these times, don't be afraid to mention their loved one; there is comfort in knowing they are remembered.

Above all, be there for them. You can help make the difference between a grief that overshadows and dominates the rest of a person's days, or a grief that, although never leaving completely, is absorbed into the fabric of their life.

# What Shall I Read Next?

### Even Though I Walk...
*Jackie Slough*

ISBN: 978-1-907509-94-0

The journey of coping with grief is unique for each person. For the author, Jackie, it began when her teenage son died. She and her family had to lean heavily on God and learn how to act, how to feel, how to respond to others and what to say when friends didn't know what to say to them. This book is a result of that journey and will help others starting out on the same road, as well as those who want to understand what the journey of grief is like so they may help their friends or family.

### Two Minus One Equals One
*Geoff Treasure*

ISBN: 978-1-907509-46-9

In this book Geoff Treasure offers hope, comfort and advice to those who are grieving the loss of a loved one, with sensitivity and understanding. Himself a widower, Geoff relates the emotions, questions and challenges common to those who are suffering with grief. Using the biblical story of Lazarus as a reference and his own experiences as examples, Geoff provides practical help and warm encouragement whilst recognising the very personal nature of suffering.